CW00346879

MONOLOGUES THAT MATTER

Contemporary Monologues for Young Actors Which Capture the Voices of Our Generation

PAMELA CASSELLS-TOTTON

authorHOUSE®

AuthorHouse™ UK
1663 Liberty Drive
Bloomington, IN 47403   USA
www.authorhouse.co.uk
Phone: 0800.197.4150

Published by AuthorHouse 11/16/2018

ISBN: 978-1-7283-8084-1 (sc)
ISBN: 978-1-7283-8083-4 (e)

Print information available on the last page.

CONTENTS

INTRODUCTION FROM THE AUTHOR

I have been writing original monologues, duologues, plays, songs and musicals for my students since I began teaching over fifteen years ago. On the drama festival circuit, when preparing students for graded examinations, or when assisting a young actor with an audition: I have always been incredibly frustrated with the limited published material available to young actors – despite the incredibly high demand for such material! The scripts, and the age-old roles for children: Annie, Oliver, Matilda, Gavroche; although brilliant and exceptional stories and characters; have grown tired and repetitive in the aforementioned arenas. My students don't want to play the same characters that they've seen on stages many times before. They want to play characters that are modern, real, hilarious, relatable. They want an audience to engage and pay attention when they perform an original piece - which has never been seen or heard before. The resulting monologues made up the collection within this book.

Over the years, I have bought countless monologue books – none of which I have felt authentically speak to or represent the lives and interests of young people. I spend a lot of time with young people, almost every single day over the past twenty years – almost – and I feel this has helped me to tune in to what motivates, engages and inspires the young people of our generation. I have written every piece in this collection true to their voice. I believe that this book will be a drama teacher's "God send" and most trusted resource. It is a one stop shop for material which will challenge students, whilst allowing them to showcase their talent through a range of dynamic characters and emotional pieces.

Each monologue in this collection has been tried and tested, revamped, edited, cut, and re-written multiple times over the past decade and beyond; and my students have not only enjoyed playing the following characters, but they have been acclaimed in their portrayal, winning awards at Festivals up and down the country, from Best Actor to Most Memorable Performance. Beyond the festival circuit the following monologues have also been used and adapted successfully for auditions to show my students' or clients' range as actors and their ability to tackle contemporary characters, conveying complexities of meaning and sophisticated interpretations. All of the above is there for the taking within the monologues which follow.

You will notice that in some of the introductions to monologues I have suggested a proposed age of the character. This is merely a guideline and should not be a limiting factor. If you have an actor you believe has the sensibility to play a certain character, do not let the stated age stand in their way.

I would like to thank the wonderful Brigid Shine for her help and support throughout the publishing process, this would not have been possible without your assistance. Not forgetting my husband who has always been my greatest inspiration to write. He notices a spark in me when I get into my flow for writing a piece of theatre and encourages me to find time to write even in my most hectic weeks with my school and my agency. For this, I thank you, Kris.

PREFACE

Pamela Cassells-Totton is a trailblazing entrepreneur, artistic director, actor's agent and writer from Northern Ireland. Pamela has spent her career transforming Performing Arts education and its impact on the young people of Northern Ireland, over the past fifteen years. Pamela's vision started out when she was just seventeen, in 2003 - with a Speech and Drama class of only four pupils. Since then, the Pamela Cassells School of Performance, or PCSP, has grown to become a stellar establishment at the heartbeat of the community, welcoming over 1000 young people through its doors over the years, and counting! PCSP plays such a pivotal role in the community; not only for its innovative, rigorous and quality Performing Arts training and outreach, but for its legacy as a cross-community initiative. PCSP brings together young people from all sides of the community, regardless of their background or beliefs. This is unique for an educational institution in Northern Ireland, where integrated education is not the norm. As artistic director of PCSP, Pamela has worked to establish a multi award-winning school of Performing Arts, operating in multiple branches, with a packed class schedule almost every day of the week. As a teacher she has a very personal approach and considers every one of her students a member of her close family. During weekly classes it is a marvel to watch how Pamela empowers her students and celebrates their individuality.

Pamela trained as an actor at Belfast Institute for Higher Education and as a dancer through the Royal Academy of Dance and British Theatre. Pamela appeared alongside Jimmy Nesbitt in ITV Drama *Cinderella*, and has fronted multiple national advertising campaigns for Tourism NI, Sunblest, the Police Service, and the Department of Education to name but a few. She has tread the boards of some of the UK's most renowned theatres, working with stellar directors and production companies such as *Cragrats*, Richard Croxford, Roma Tumelty, Stephen Kelly and the late, great, Peter Quigley.

Throughout her teenage years, Pamela worked as a missionary, and ever since, has always been an activist, championing causes of those less fortunate. Even in its youth, it was Pamela's mission that PCSP would inspire students and their families with the power of the Arts as a force for change. Pamela worked extensively as an actor, and then director and writer, with leading theatre in education companies *Cragrats* and *c21*, witnessing how their work was having a massive impact on young audiences. In recent years, Pamela decided to combine her passion for creating powerful issue-based theatre, with the talented students in her ranks, to create a theatre company. Their united aim is to provide a platform for young voices to be heard, and stories to be told, while shining a light on the serious issues facing young people today. Over the past number of years PCSP have collaborated with the Children's Commissioner, the Department of Education, the Police Force of Northern Ireland and a multitude of community organisations and charities to produce critically acclaimed, award-winning productions *The Current, Carousel, 24, Two Sides of the Same Coin* which have toured multiple theatres and venues throughout Northern Ireland reaching out to young audiences. Where many people today shy away from the issues on the streets, Pamela works tirelessly to face them head on. She is passionate about verbatim theatre and creating work that will tell real stories about real people. Rehearsals are always a collaborative process and PCSP students have free reign to create the type of theatre they would want to see; telling stories they believe their peers need to hear.

The immense talent within the ranks of PCSP students is a great sense of pride within the local community. Pamela, as an actor herself, knows how difficult it can be to get a break in the industry, has always strived to equip those students who want to pursue a career in the arts with the best possible training, opportunities, insight and contacts. It is in her pursuit of arming her students for the industry that she noticed that there was no quality representation for young people in Northern Ireland - even though the TV/Film production industry has experienced a boom in the country in recent years. There was nothing else for it. *Rising Talent* was born, with Pamela at the helm. Rising Talent has over fifty young actors on its books and in the agency's short life, actors have starred in countless national and international TV and film productions including *Game of Thrones* (HBO), *Paula, The Fall, My Mother and Other Strangers, Come Home, The Secret* (BBC), *Grace and Goliath* (NI Screen/Cinemagic); as well as countless theatrical credits throughout Northern Ireland.

When not running one of her three companies, Pamela loves to write. Alongside renowned UK composer, Mark Dougherty, Pamela has been commissioned by theatre company c21 multiple times to write musicals, Christmas shows and pantomimes, *Strive the Musical; Lucy and the Dreamcatcher; Aladdin; Jack and the Beanstalk; Snow White and the Seven Hallions.* Her productions have enjoyed sell-out runs in multiple theatres, and critical acclaim. Pamela has also worked on the creative teams within *GBL Productions, LANA Production*s, and *c21 Theatre Company* as Director, Associate Director and Associate Choreographer.

MONOLOGUES FOR PRE-TEEN ACTORS

FIRST DATE

In this scene, eight-year-old Tommy gets ready for his first date.

TOMMY. Okay, so let's do a quick check. Teeth brushed. *(Checks his breath.)* Yes, minty fresh! Hair combed, yes - and perfectly styled. Fresh underwear... *(Checks.)* Yes, clean, just out of the wash!

Hi, Sarah, how are you keeping today? No, too formal. What's happenin'? No, too...street! Hi, Mrs Right. Somebody said you were looking for me. Mmm...yeah. I think that might work.

Sarah's a girl from my school who has clearly fancied me for ages. I fancy her too. But I heard on TV it's important to play hard to get, so I've been doing that and haven't really spoken to her in a while. But we're off for half term, so I thought it was a promising idea to finally ask her out on a date. She said yes—of course. Dad phoned her mum, and it's all sorted. My dad's a legend. He gave me loads of useful tips and even lent me his aftershave. I hope I didn't pour too much on. *(shrugs)*. Only about half the bottle, but I still can't smell it. Dad gave me money so I can pay her way in and buy some popcorn. That's bound to impress her I reckon. Although I hope she doesn't like popcorn that much 'cause I'm starving. Dad said we should watch a romantic film as Sarah would love that, but there's no way I'm heading to the cinema to watch a chick flick. Imagine if someone saw me!

Another thing Dad said was to always remember my manners. I agree, so I've decided to wait until ten minutes in, when the lights go out, before I try to kiss her. I'm going to try the wee trick. You know, the one where you pretend to yawn, but you're really doing it so you can put your arm round someone. Then I'm going in for the kiss!

THE TOOTH FAIRY

Toolip is one of the many tooth fairies who has been feeling overworked and underpaid. She speaks directly to the audience.

TOOLIP. Only one more hour until my shift starts. Great, another night of torture. I need a holiday... and a pay rise. Seriously, it's like slave labour around here. Each night we start at eight. We're given our schedule and sent out into the dark night. It's a nightmare trying to find all the addresses, especially when my satnav loses signal! By the time we've been to all our calls and flown back to Fairy Land, it's eight in the morning, and we are knackered. A full twelve-hour shift with no breaks. Surely there is a law against that, right?

Everyone thinks we fairies have the life of it, skipping around in pretty dresses, sprinkling dust everywhere we go. Well let me tell you, looks can be deceiving. There is nothing glamourous about this job.

First of all, we have to fly for hours on end, the equivalent to running a marathon in your world. Would you fancy doing that every night? Didn't think so!

Then, whilst flying, we must carry around a huge bag of pound coins to slip under children's pillows. Have you ever felt the weight of a huge bag of coins? I've had serious back pain for years. We keep hoping our boss will upgrade the lost tooth rate to fivers, which would be much easier to carry. But no sign of that yet.

Next, we have to lift old teeth with our *bare hands*. Have you ever thought about how gross that is? And some of them aren't in the best condition. Really not pleasant.

Sometimes kids wake up when they feel their pillows moving, and we have to hide out in their rooms until they fall asleep again. That can be terrifying, not to mention the fact it can hold up our whole schedule and leave us way behind.

When we do get back to Fairy Land, we are so exhausted that we just sleep for most of the day. What kind of life is that?

I've applied for other fairy posts and filled in so many application forms. But the positions are all filled. I keep waiting for some of them to retire. I mean, let's face it; they've been around for a long time. Take Puck, for example. Or Tink. It's about time those two started to slow down and give this tooth fairy a lucky break.

GET RICH QUICK

In this scene, smart and quirky Ruby is fed up with her parents, siblings, and well, pretty much life in general. Here, she fantasises about becoming a superhero and ruling the world.

RUBY. *(Enters, gives her brother some sass.)* Whatever, Timmy. Yeah, yeah, yeah. I triple dare you to. Wimp.

(Addresses the audience.) Brothers are soooo annoying, and immature and *boring*! In fact, so are sisters and mothers and fathers. And just about everyone who lives in this house.

It's always, 'Ruby, it's past your bedtime'. 'Ruby came into my room again, Mum'. 'Ruby, love, you're too young to watch this programme. Maybe when you're older'. Bla, bla, bla! I hate being the youngest. No one thinks I am capable of anything around here.

What if there was a way to show them, show them my full potential? Show them I'm a force to be reckoned with.

Imagine if I were a superhero with superhero powers!

I could be called Rock Star Ruby. No, not flashy enough. Racey Road Runner. No, too obvious. I've got it now—Rocket Rubster. Yeah, I like it!

Rocket Rubster, whose powers would be unlimited. At any point in time I could transport myself from one place to another. So whenever Mum and Dad got too much, *zoom,* and I'd be gone! Amazing. Just imagine their faces.

Then *KAPOW, BLAM, ZAP a*nd Timothy gets it right in the nose! That ought to teach him a lesson or two.

I could take over the school. My intelligence would be so impressive that I would sack the principal and give everyone a few weeks off. Then when they all came back, surprise, the school would be transformed into a massive play arena. It would have skate parks, ice rinks, cinemas...the lot. Then I would be a true hero and move on to take over the world.

I can just see the headlines: 'Rocket Rubster Conquers the World!'

Now, just to sneak into Timmy's room and snatch his laptop. I need to get on Google. Google knows everything, and there's just bound to be a step-by-step guide to becoming a superhero.

Here I goooooooooooo... Rocket Rubster!

FAST FORWARD

This play is set during the troubles in Northern Ireland during the late twentieth century. It is told through the innocent eyes of children growing up during the Troubles. Edwina—Winnie—is nine years old. It's just gone 10 p.m., and she is alone in the house.

WINNIE. *(Sitting on the floor, playing snakes and ladders.)* Ach, it's no fun playing on your own. There's no real point to it. I love competition; I always win. Well, I always beat my mummy, but sometimes daddy beats me. Although I swear he cheats because he's always got that sneaky wee look on his face. The same look he has when Mummy tells us we aren't allowed to eat any more of the Jacob's biscuits because there are hardly any left. But Daddy always steals us two. He's so much fun.

That's where my Mummy went. *(She gets up and moves to the window.)* Away to look for my daddy. She says it's like an adult game of hide-and-seek, and she has to find him. He left in a rush earlier

9

tonight. He just came running downstairs in his big black coat and hat, gave me a wee wink like this *(She demonstrates.)* and then left. He does that a lot. Sometimes Mummy just shakes her head and looks worried. Then she goes to the back door and smokes like a hundred cigarettes. But tonight, Mummy said she had to go after him and find him 'cause they were playing hide-and-seek. She locked me in here but promised when they came back, we could play hide-and-seek together. But that wouldn't be much fun 'cause there's nowhere to hide in here!

(She looks out the window again.) There's the police—again! They are always up and down this street. And look at that smoke. Class! There seems to be loads going on tonight. That would be so brilliant for a game of hide-and-seek.

(She goes back to the game but is obviously bored.)

I am sooo bored! I hate being on my own; it's boring. *(Winnie hears what sounds like a gunshot.)* What's that? Someone must have been shot again.

(Winnie continues to play the game, singing to herself. Then she hears her mother outside.)

I can hear Mummy. *(She jumps up and goes to the window.)* There she is! *(Pauses briefly.)* She's cry - Why is my mummy crying?

(Winnie calls out to her and bangs on the window.) Mummy, mummy, what's wrong? Stop crying. Where's daddy? Mummy! Mummy, stop crying! Where's my daddy?

HOME SWEET HOME

Maddie is seven years old and has decided to run away from home. She has brought nothing on her journey but a backpack filled with 'essentials'. She speaks directly to the audience.

MADDIE. It's official. I've done it. I've ran away from home!

This has been a long time in planning and has taken a lot of precision, but I made it. And I have packed for every possible outcome. Yes, I am fully equipped and eternally happy. I am free!

No more nagging from mum and dad, no more homework, no more early mornings. I can go to bed when I like, eat ice cream when I like, and watch YouTube all day long if I fancy it. This is the best decision I have ever made.

I just couldn't stick living at home anymore. No one listens to me, no one appreciates me. I've tried for seven whole years now to get along with those people, but they just don't give me the respect I deserve, and well, I'm at the end of my tether with the lot of them. I have decided to become independent. I am perfectly capable of looking after myself. Anyway, they probably won't even notice I'm gone. Mum and dad will be too busy fussing over baby Jess to even realise I'm not there. I swear, you'd think she was the Queen the way they treat her, and all she does is eat, cry, and... and...the other thing! You know what I mean. I just don't know what the big deal is with her.

Anyway, I think I'll sit down and rest my feet. I need to have a look at my schedule. This bag is a tonne weight! *(She sits and rummages through her bag.)*

Where is my schedule? Maybe under my roller skates. *(She lifts out a roller boot.)* You never know when you'll need a quick getaway. Ah, there it is. *(She reads the schedule.)*

Okay, what time is it? 4.15p.m. 'Have a much-needed rest.' Tick, I'm doing that now! 4.30pm 'Make sure to eat!' Good idea, I am really hungry. Where's my packed lunch? *(She rummages in the bag.)* It's got to be in here somewhere. I definitely put it in - I'm sure of it. *(She searches the backpack more frantically.)*

No way, no lunch box! How could I be so careless? Not to worry. I've got my purse, and I'll walk on a bit further. It shouldn't be that far to Mc Donald's, probably only about 10 miles or so. That will only take me about...five minutes, I'm sure.

Right, where is my purse? *(She finds it in the backpack, opens it and tips it upside down.)* You have got to be kidding me. I definitely had money in there yesterday. Timothy must have stolen it without me knowing. He is dead meat! Brothers are so annoying!

Now what am I going to do? I've no lunch box, and no money. I'll just have to starve to death. That'll show them I mean business. *(Pause)*

Oh no, did you hear that? My belly is rumbling. What day is it today? Saturday. My favourite. Spaghetti Bolognese night. My mum makes the best Bolognese. And the X-factor is on at eight...I wonder who will be voted out tonight?

Maybe I could just nip home for dinner and the X-factor, then run away again tomorrow. I think that might work. No point trying to run away on an empty stomach. And it is getting a bit cold out here. One last night with my electric blanket should do the trick, then I'll be much more prepared in the morning.

Yes, that's what I'll do. I'll try and put up with them all for one more night, and I'll most definitely, without a doubt, run away forever, tomorrow!

Now...let's get me some spag bol...!

LENT

In this scene, nine-year-old Kerry has made a Lenten promise she is not sure she can keep.

KERRY. I've gone off sweets for lent.

My mum is making me do it. I'm totally forced into it. Why would I ever want to do something like this to myself? It's like some sort of torture. Forty long days, and forty sleepless nights. Craving. Longing...for just a few Haribo, or some delicious Skittles...mmmmm.

Honestly, I think my Mum needs to re-evaluate her parenting skills. This is no way to treat her only daughter. She keeps saying things like 'This is an opportunity for reflection Kerry'. What does that even mean?

Fair enough, I know Jesus went into the desert to fast and pray, but, hello? That's Jesus, he has super powers, right? I'm just little old Kerry, and I want sweets. I've figured that I still have a few options. Chocolate buttons, Minstrels, Maltesers... See, I would class those as chocolate, wouldn't you?

There is absolutely no way they are sweets. Mum insisted I go off sweets, but she never mentioned chocolate, so I'm sweet! *(She realises what she has said.)* ...Sweet...

This is driving me insane. I can feel a headache coming on. And no one likes Kerry with a headache.

Plus, it's Bella's birthday at the weekend, and she's having a sleepover. How socially awkward am I going to look if I can't eat sweets with everyone? Clearly my Mum hasn't thought about the lasting effects this could have on my life. Goodness, this could even result in bullying!

Mum and I need a chat - immediately. Surely, she will be impressed with my willpower so far and maybe draw a line in the sand, and call it quits. It has been 4 hours and 26 minutes after all. That's impressive!

FAIRY WISHES

Noelle is a Christmas Fairy who lives atop a Christmas tree. She explains what life is like at the top of the tree during the festive season.

NOELLE. Oh, I am fed up I can tell you. You see, I'm the fairy at the top of the Christmas tree. You know the one, don't you? I make my appearance once a year, then I'm stuffed back in a horrible, dark box and stored in a very creepy attic. How can anyone treat a fairy with such little respect? And then, once a year when I do get my moment to shine, no one in this house really cares that much anyway!

There's Derek, the father of the Smith family. He takes a big swig of something that smells horrible, then he wibbles and wobbles on a stool trying to get me to the top. It always takes a few attempts.

Then, all the family stand around the tree clapping and cheering, looking up at me with admiration... It lasts all of about thirty seconds. Thirty seconds! Then I blend into total insignificance while they go back to the hustle and bustle of their lives. No one talks to me, no one looks at me... I may as well not be there.

You'd be surprised at what goes on at the Smith's. It has shocked this fairy to her core - I can tell you that much. Tom and Daisy Smith - that's the kids - are always arguing and chasing each other. They're not very nice. Just two nights before Santa's arrival, Derek had quite a large glass of red wine sitting by the fireside. He had moaned and groaned about eating too much at dinner – (*whispers*) he is really rather large - and he left, presumably for the not-so-little men's room. Next thing, the kids came barging in, Tom yelling that Daisy was going to get coal on Christmas morning for being horrible, smelly and irritating. Two of the three are quite accurate, but of course I never said.

Anyway, they were running around the room when Daisy tripped over. She kicked Daddy's precious glass of red wine all over Mummy dearest's gloriously white carpet. Instantly they panicked, then joined forces like they'd never been fighting in the first place. They started shifting presents, then the Christmas tree, which meant that *I* was being moved abruptly. My halo, my wings, shaking all over the place. It was like a military operation. Tom was shouting instructions like a sergeant, while Daisy dutifully obeyed. Listening and responding to each other in a very effective way. Finally, the stain had been covered and the problem solved... so they went straight back to bickering again!

When Derek returned, he looked at the glass and stalled for a moment...before going to refill it.

Meanwhile Mummy Smith is cleaning and scrubbing and washing and drying. The house is always spotless. I didn't know it was possible to do so much cleaning. Sometimes she looks like she is cleaning away all the problems in the world. Well, her world. I like Mrs Smith. I feel sorry for her.

Alas, Christmas is now over. I was lucky to get one extra day this year, before the Smiths got fed up with all the Christmas decorations. They packed us all up and shoved us back into this cold, dark attic. Oh, to see another season. Oh, to be free! I guess every Christmas fairy can dream.

JAB

Eight-year-old Claire sits in the queue waiting to get the flu jab.

CLAIRE. Oh great. There are only five more people in front of me. Then I must face the music, meet my fate. I am dreading this. I don't think it's one bit fair. It's my body. Surely, I should be the one to decide if I want to get stabbed in the arm or not. I hate injections. Have you seen the size of those needles? And normally the nurses aren't nice at all, they're all liars! *'It will be over in a flash...just look the other way and you won't feel a thing'.* Yeah right. How can I not feel a thing when you stick a 6-inch needle into my tiny little arm?

(She looks at her arm.) I'm sorry arm, I really am. If I had a choice, me and you would be out of here. Wait, maybe we could do a runner, what do you think? The issue is getting past Killer Carson. She is the meanest teacher in the school. I heard that she once locked a boy in her store for over *four* hours, and she got away with it. Apparently,

she lives in a big house in the middle of nowhere and always has the blinds closed. They reckon she has dead bodies in there. Maybe not the best idea to get caught doing a runner or it will be more than an arm I might lose.

I begged my Mum to write me a sick note today or let me stay off school. Of course, she said no. Great moral support or what? I'd take the flu any day of the week before having to put myself through this torture. I don't mind coughing and spluttering for a few days. I'd even take the red nose just to avoid this pain! One more person then it's me. No getting out of this now. I'm starting to feel warm...and a bit dizzy... Oh no, it's my turn. Coming now. Just give me a sec...oh... *(She faints. After a few seconds she lifts her head up, with one eye open.)*

Oh Miss Carson, hi... What do you mean you don't believe me? Okay, okay I'm going now. Sorry arm. *(She sulks off.)*

CSI: THE THREE BEARS

In this scene Baby Bear is being interviewed by a Police Officer. Baby Bear has been asked to give a statement about an incident that occurred in his home.

BABY BEAR. How many times do I have to go through this officer? You're wasting valuable time when you should be out catching this villain!

Let me break it down for you one more time. Dad, mum, and I returned home after a long morning walking in the forest. We were tired and hungry. We came into the house as we usually do, but the minute we got inside, we knew something wasn't right. Call it animal instinct if you like, but we just sensed it. Dad rushed over to the kitchen table and noticed that someone had been eating his porridge... *Big* mistake in our house. No one ever touches dad's food. It's a serious no-no. When mum went to him to calm him down, she noticed someone had been nibbling at her porridge too. I mean, what is going on here? They both looked at my bowl, then looked to me. I knew this could only mean one thing. Someone had eaten my porridge too. All of it!

What sort of creature would come into our house and polish off our porridge like that? Dad was on the rampage. He rushed into the living room, nearly taking the door off its hinges, and bellowed, *'Someone's been sitting on my chair!'*

Mum noticed the same. Then me. That crook had left my chair shattered into pieces. My only chair that my dad had built for me. In the evenings, after long days out in the forest, the three of us always relax on our chairs, while dad melts marshmallows by the fire. Mum sits knitting, and dad tells me stories of when he was a young bear. How can we do that now, when I have no chair?

After this, the three of us crept upstairs. It's not easy to creep when you're a bear, but dad told us to be silent. When we got to the top dad saw that someone had been lying on his bed. Mum saw that someone had been lying on her bed. And as I have told you officer, three times now, a girl, a real girl, with long golden hair was in *my* bed! I can't remember exactly what happened after that. All I know is, she woke up, screamed, and went running out of our house.

You need to find her, officer, immediately. She needs to be caught and punished for what she has done. *(Beat.)*

What do you mean our stories don't add up? In what way does it sound like a 'fairytale'? If you don't find this Goldilocks chick soon...then WE WILL!

TRANSFORMATION

While her Mum was at work, nine-year-old Becky decided to give herself a make-over. It didn't go according to plan. Her mum is furious, and Becky tries to pacify her.

BECKY. Calm down, Mum. Cool the jets...chill out! Please stop yelling at me before you burst a blood vessel. I get it. You're angry and I'm grounded.

Look, I really am sorry. I just, you know, fancied a change. I just got sick of the same old face and hair staring back at me. Plus, my style was so dated, so ordinary. Long, straight, dark brown hair...boring. At least this funky little bob is cute, fresh.

That didn't help, did it? I just want you to understand, that's all. I know I shouldn't have used your hair dye, and perhaps I did leave it on a bit too long. But I'm inexperienced at this sort of thing. I'll make a better job of it next time. I mean...of *course* I won't try something like this again.

In fairness though, Mum...I kind of thought you'd understand. You change your hair all the time. Goodness knows how many colours you've had over the years. Obviously you need to do that to cover the greys, but I also think you love a change as much as me. And celebrities, hello? They change their hairstyle more often than their underwear!

I know you're angry, but admit it...you think it's cool, don't you? I look like a rockstar and you know it. Inside you're probably smiling at how creative I've been, and you're probably inspired to go for something a little more edgy yourself, aren't you? Instead of that bob you keep getting that makes you look older than you are.

For all we know Mum, maybe this is what I was born to do. I could be a hairdresser in the making, and you're grounding me for practicing my craft. I think I have quite a natural flair for this. Sure, I know that it might not be cut completely even, but it's hard to see the back of your head.

Wait! I've just had a brainwave... Since I'm going to be grounded and really bored, maybe I could practice on you, Mum? How do you fancy a pink Mohican? I think you could really pull that off. Shall I get my scissors?

MARCHING ORDERS

Becky has lived for the past few years within the foster care system. She rarely talks about her real parents, but when she does it always leaves her feeling at rock bottom. In this scene she speaks with one of her senior counsellors, Lucille, whom she feels very close to.

BECKY. I really don't mind. Honestly, it doesn't bother me either way. It did in the past, but now I'm used to it. Remember a few years back when I got that nice family that lived in the country? Anne and Ronnie, remember? And they had the big black and white dog. What breed was he again? I can't remember. Did I tell you that Ronnie was a dog breeder? He had all these books with pictures of dogs that told you all about their breeds. I used to sit up on his knee and he'd read them to me. It was fascinating.

I hated it when they gave me up. I wanted to stay there forever.

It bothered me at the time. But not now. You see I've hardened, toughened up. *(She jumps up acting the clown.)* Look, watch me flex my muscles. I'm a toughie now! *(Laughing at her own silliness.)* Plus, it's probably for the best that I'm moving on from the Lennon's. I understand why they've said they can't have me anymore, but I want you to know it wasn't my fault, Lucille. I want you to know the truth. I don't care what they think, but I need to know you believe me.

I told you, when you came to visit me about a month ago, that Elsa, their real daughter, is not what she seems. You see, she acts all prim and proper in front of her mummy and daddy, and sits up in church on a Sunday with a sweet little smile on her face, but inside? She's the devil. I'm sorry. I know I shouldn't say that, but it's true. She was always saying stuff to me about how I was a reject, how her family didn't really want me there. She'd say that no one wanted me. Bla bla bla. I'd heard that all before from others. That's what I mean when I say I'm hardened to it.

But last week before, the 'incident', she brought up my mum and dad. No one ever does that. They are mine to talk about and to think about. No one else's.

Anyway, she started asking about the accident. I could feel my face getting redder and redder. I felt like I was going to explode. She said that her mum told her that my dad had been drinking but drove the car anyway with my mum and wee Jay in it. I know that's not true. My dad would never do that.

She said that she wished I had been in the car too and then all my family would be dead, and no one would have to pretend to like me anymore.

She just...kept saying stuff and it just got too much for me. My ears started to buzz, my eyes went blurry and I just lost it, Lucille. I lost it and started lashing out. And...well you know the rest.

(Starts to break down.) I'm sorry. I'm so sorry, Lucille. But she should never have mentioned my parents and Jay. No one should. They are mine to talk about, no one else. I'm sorry.

Where will I go now Lucille?

DEEP BREATH

Ten-year-old Grace was involved in a very bad car accident and is now in a coma. This play looks at the lives of those affected by this awful tragedy, and how they each deal with grief differently. In this scene we meet Georgia, Grace's best friend. Grace's family have decided that they can't bear to watch their daughter suffer like this for a moment longer. This will be the last time that Georgia will see Grace.

GEORGIA. *(Enters and sits down at the hospital bed.)*
I don't know what to say, Grace. Why don't I know what to say? I always know what to say. Can you hear me? How do I know that you're listening?

Your mum told me to be brave and come in to say goodbye to you. I don't know how to be brave anymore. I don't know how to be anything anymore. *(She gets angry, defiant.)* Anyway, what's the point of saying goodbye if you can't hear me? There's no point. It's stupid. Pathetic! *(Beat.)*

I'm sorry. I shouldn't have said that. That was selfish. Of course you can hear me. You're probably lying there thinking, *'I wish Georgia would stop blabbering on and get to the point'.*

You always used to say that to me. I'd be excited to tell you a story about what happened in class that week, or about my brother's friend Pete who always leaves me those stupid notes, and you'd always stop me mid flow and say, *'Stop blabbering Georgia and get to the point!'* You just wanted to hear the juicy bit of the story right away; you had no patience for my dramatic build up.

I will miss that about you.

I'll miss everything about you. The sound of your goofy laugh, the way you stuff your face with pepperoni pizza, our pretend fashion shows ... No one will ever be you. No one will ever make me laugh the way you do.

Why do you have to go Georgia? Why wasn't I with you that day? Why do I have to say goodbye to the only friend I've ever had? Why? *(Breaks down.)* None of this is fair, none of it seems real.

(Georgia takes a deep breath.)

I guess I have to go now. Your family are outside waiting.

Goodbye Grace, I'll never forget you. Never.

MONOLOGUES FOR TEENAGE ACTORS

JUST ME?

Luke has always felt different to the rest of his peers. In this scene he addresses the audience directly about his favourite pastime.

LUKE. *(Luke is putting on make-up.)* I bet you think I'm weird, yeah? A thirteen-year-old boy sitting in his bedroom putting on make-up. Why is this so weird to people though? I'm perfectly fine about it. Doesn't everyone have the right to be themselves? Do what makes them happy?

(He stands up, facing the audience.)

I'm Luke. I'm thirteen years old and I enjoy wearing make-up and dressing up in girl's clothes sometimes. What's the big deal? *(He sings dramatically.)* 'I am what I am, I am my own special creation...' and all that!

I've always loved make-up and dressing up for as long as I can remember. Even as a toddler I loved playing with girl's toys. Pink has always been my favourite colour, always. My favourite thing, as a child, was when mum went to pick dad up from work in the evenings. Every night when she'd leave, I had the journey from our house to dad's work timed to perfection. It took exactly seventeen minutes. As soon as the front door closed, and mum got into the car, I would rush upstairs and go straight to her wardrobe. I'd pick out one of her dresses and a pair of high heels, quickly get them on and examine my reflection in the mirror. Then I'd parade around the house pretending to be a supermodel. With about three minutes to spare I'd get back into my own clothes and sprint back downstairs again before you could say tranny. Oh, the adrenalin of it all was amazing, electrifying. Each night I'd leave it a split second longer because the buzz of getting caught was so exhilarating.

Dad left us a few years ago, met someone else. So, it's just me and Mum now. She knows now, about my...hobby, and she's great. Sometimes we have pamper nights and give each other facials and stuff.

I get the impression that she feels if she allows me to be the way I want to be in the safety of our home, she can protect me from the rest of the world. The thing is, I don't want to hide it. Why should I? I'm comfortable just being me. It's everyone else's issue, not mine.

So, world...brace yourself. 'Cause here I am!

ABC

Maddie goes to a private school and has lots of friends. One of her friends, Emily, has had to move school due to severe bullying and Maddie is feeling guilty that she didn't speak up and defend her.

MADDIE. The dictionary definition of courage is: 'To do something even though it scares you.'

I do things all the time that scare me. I got up in front of my entire year and made a speech about recycling. That terrified me. But I did it. I once walked from Claire's house to mine in pitch black darkness. I was terrified, but again, I did it. I even kissed Ross from my history class at the school disco. The butterflies in my stomach were going crazy...but I did it. I do have courage.

So why didn't I tell Melissa and her cronies to back off and leave Emily alone? It's not because I'm afraid of Melissa. 'Cause I'm not. It's because I wanted everyone to like me. How selfish. Me, me, me. The world revolves around me. I need to learn to put other people first. So many times, I stood back and watched them pick on Emily, and I said nothing. Nothing! I just pretended it wasn't happening and fooled myself into thinking that Emily was going to be fine.

She had a 'breakdown'. At least that's what Miss Birch called it. A twelve-year-old having a breakdown. What does that even mean? No one has seen her since and there are all sorts of rumours about what school she will go to. I tried phoning her, but her number must be changed. Anyway, what would I say? Sorry, Emily, that I was too selfish to speak up. Sorry I stood back and did nothing while you were treated like that? Bit late now. She'd probably hang up. I wouldn't blame her.

Ever since it happened I can't get it out of my head. I feel responsible. Sure, I might not have said all the nasty things, but I listened and did nothing. And that makes me as bad as them.

BRAVE FACE

Aaron is being bullied. He doesn't confide in anyone about it and feels very alone. He is in his bedroom preparing to go to school.

AARON. *(Enters, packing his school books, fixing his tie and hair etc.)*

Monday morning. The time I dread.

I know most kids dread Monday's. The weekend is over, and all the week ahead brings is homework, early mornings and uniforms. I dread all that too, but that's not all. I sort of get picked on. Bullied, in a way, I suppose. Although it isn't that bad. I haven't ever got attacked or had bruises or anything. So, I suppose I shouldn't really complain. Some kids get it a lot worse than me.

It's this group of boys in my school. They are part of the 'in' gang. Everyone wants to be like them, look like them. You are regarded as "super cool" if you hang out with them. There is no doubt about it. They are pretty cool and popular. And I guess I am just different.

You see, I love reading and art. Recently I drew this picture of the bridge near where I live. It was a Sunday afternoon and I was stuffed after lunch. I took myself off for a walk- I always bring my backpack with whatever book I am reading, and my sketchpad. That particular day, the sun was shining and whatever way it landed on the water it just looked incredible. It would have made the perfect photograph for a postcard. So, I tried my best to capture it.

The next day I brought it into school to show my art teacher. She was so impressed she said she would enter it into the County School's art competition where the winner gets £100 and a ticket to this cool exhibition at City Hall. I was over the moon. At break I was showing the picture to one of the girls from my class when Josh and his gang came over. They grabbed it off me and made me watch while they tore it up.

That's what they're like. They mock me, laugh at me, push me around, and basically make my life a living hell.

I know it's probably my own fault. I should be stronger and stand up to them, but it's hard. And I can't exactly tell anyone can I? *'Josh ripped up my picture'* or *'Josh and his gang laughed at me'.* I would sound so childish and stupid!

It's just... I feel so miserable...and lonely. And sometimes scared. Scared that they are round the next corner waiting for me. They are always there no matter where I turn, and every night they are in my nightmares. It just makes me feel like giving up.

Pathetic, I know. I guess I just have to pretend like everything is okay and put on a brave face.

(Finishes packing up, takes a deep breath and exits.)

PIROUETTE

In this scene we meet Sofia. She has been mustering the confidence to have this conversation with her Mum for weeks. She has finally plucked up the courage to confront her.

SOFIA. Morning Mum. I need to chat to you about something, if that's okay? Is now a good time?
    (Her mum responds.) Do you want to sit down?
    (Sofia takes a deep breath.) Firstly, I want you to know how grateful I am for the training you have given me over the years. You are the most beautiful dancer I have ever seen, and you really inspire me. Sometimes, I stop and think to myself about the incredible career you've had, all the famous stages you've danced on, and it takes my breath away. The discipline you have, with your training, and your diet! Goodness knows how you've managed to resist crisps and cakes and the yummy things I love to eat. The physical pain you've put your body through... I mean, look at your feet! No offence.

Anyway, what I'm trying to say is, I think you're amazing, I really do. You've taught me so much about ballet, and you've trained me to become a great dancer too, and for that I'll be forever grateful.

But, the thing is... Ballet is not what I want to do with my life. It's not my dream. I know that you have high hopes for my career as a dancer, but it's not what I want. I know the time and energy you've invested in me, and I'm sorry if I'm letting you down, I really am. I've been so worried about telling you. I've been putting it off, but that's been unfair of me. I know that you've been speaking to some of your contacts. I overheard you on the phone talking to Miss Keenan at the Royal Ballet School, and well, I thought it best to tell you now before this got out of control.

I really love dancing, I do. But it's just not what I want to do with my life. *(She tries to lighten the mood.)* Plus, you and I both know, I'd never survive without chocolate! *(Beat.)* I hope you understand Mum? Please don't cry...

'OH, TO BE YOUNG AGAIN...'

In this scene Brigid goes to Confession.

BRIGID. Hello, Father. I hope you're keeping well? The chapel's looking great, has it had a wee revamp? *(No response.)* That's very bad weather we've been having, isn't it? My Aunt Katherine's house... *(Priest interrupts.)*

Oh yes, Father. My sins. You're right, sorry Father, forgive me. Right... Here goes... *(Beat.)*

What do I have to say again, Father? *(She listens.)* Ah, there we are Father, thanks. I was just testing you! Right, so...

Forgive me Father for you have sinned, I mean...I have sinned. It has been so long since my last confession.

(Priest interrupts.) Oh right, I have to say how long it's been since my last confession? Got ya. It has been sooooooo long since my last confession.

Okay. Will I go?

(There is a long pause where she is thinking hard.) Father, as you and I know it's important to

42

be honest. If I'm being completely honest, I am wracking my brain trying to think of my sins, and I can't seem to remember any. That's why I haven't been here in an age, because I don't think I need to be forgiven. But of course, my Auntie Eimear had to poke her ugly aul nose in when she was round at our house the other night. You see, her daughter is the same age as me, Patricia. Perfect Patricia. Honestly, everyone thinks the sun shines out of her a... Anyway, Patricia comes to mass every Sunday and sits there like a saint. Sure, you probably know her Father, Patricia Mc Kenna? *(He doesn't answer.)*

Well, let me tell you a thing or two about our Patricia. In school, she's a demon. She's really nasty to all the junior girls, and she meets up with Seamy McCann at lunch time and kisses him round the back of the bicycle sheds. I swear she does. I'm not one to gossip Father but if she doesn't watch out she'll get herself a bad name. My Auntie Eimear can't see her nose despite her face and she thinks her wee Patricia's perfect. So, she was bumming and blowing about Patricia the other night, she was talking about mass and how devoted they were; and asked mummy when we were last here. So of course, Mummy felt rotten and forced me to come tonight, and says we'll be back on Sunday.

I don't mean to offend you, Father, but mass is so boring. I bet you're bored to tears too. Only for the fact you're getting paid so well you probably

43

wouldn't come yourself. You must admit, it does go on a bit? If you've been to one you've been to them all, wouldn't you say?

You're very quiet in there, Father, you haven't gone to sleep have ya? The only time I'm quiet is in school when we're doing an exam. We're not allowed to speak. You're nearly afraid to breathe in case you get your head bit off. We had an exam today, Father. I think it went well. You see, I came up with a genius plan, do you want to hear it?

Well, I have a tin pencil case and when you open it the lid sits upright. So, I wrote all my answers on a wee bit of paper at home and stuck it on the inside of the pencil case. Then, before I went into the exam, I said a wee prayer to God to help me get through the exam without any of the teachers seeing that I was reading the answers. And sure enough, Father, I walked in there, sat down, opened my pencil case and answered every question perfectly. It really is incredible how God answers prayers to his faithful.

I'm just checking the time, Father for I've to go and get ready. I'm heading out tonight to a disco in the Orange Hall up in Glenny Street. There are loads of people going to it, I've been looking forward to it all week. My cousin Maeve is lending me her ID because she's got the same colour hair as me, so hopefully I'll be grand.

So, I'll be seeing you, Father. I promise I'll come back more often. Maybe next time I'll actually have a few sins to confess. Anyway, it was nice to catch up. And don't worry Father, I forgive you for not really talking much to me, you're probably talked out. I'm sure if you say a few Hail Mary's, God will forgive you too. Bye Father!

OUTSIDE LOOKING IN

Pete has just been expelled from school for getting into a fight with another student in his year. His Mum is furious and has asked him to explain his actions.

PETE. Mum, please calm down. Give me a chance to explain. Please Mum, I'm begging you. Sit down and calm yourself and let me explain.

I know I've let you down. I've let myself down, and I'm truly sorry, I am. I promise you I won't let these two weeks out of school affect my grades. I'll work extra hard to prove to you how sorry I am.

I know how bad this looks. I know you're worried about what everyone will say, and I'm sorry for that. But trust me, mum. Everyone knows you, they know how great a person you are and how well you've brought us up. You're the best mum I know. What you've done for Charlie... I don't know anyone else that could hold down a job and look after a child with Down's Syndrome single-handedly, I really don't. Not to mention looking after me as well. You're incredible Mum, and I don't say that enough. *(Doing his best to charm her.)* I know you probably think I'm only saying that to sweeten you up, but I'm not, I swear.

Anyway, I got in a fight. Yes, I got suspended for two weeks. But hear me out... Please?

We were in PE, and we were practicing the long jump to see who would qualify for sports day. Everything was fine, nothing out of the ordinary. I've told you before about Jonty and Simon and those lads. They think they're hard and they throw their weight around from time to time. They prey on the weak. To be fair, they've never got to me before. I think living with Charlie has made me thick skinned. You know what he's like, brutally honest or what?

Anyway, they sometimes wind me up about handing in homework on time, or getting good results in a test, that sort of thing, and I just brush it off. Water off a duck's back. But today when I was doing the trial, whatever way I jumped, I fell really awkwardly and made some sort of weird noise apparently. I didn't even realise I had as it all happened so quickly. Jonty yelled over, *'Now we know where his wee brother gets it from, Pete's deformed too!'*

They all laughed hysterically, and I just lost it. I saw red. I charged over to him and I was yelling and punching him. I don't even remember what happened, Mum, I really don't. I just lost it, I just lost the plot. How dare he speak about Charlie like that? How dare he ever say that?

I'd do it again. I would. I'm sorry, I know that's not what you want to hear, but it's the truth. If I was in that situation again and he started to shout his mouth off about Charlie, I'd do it again.

I'm sorry. I'm sorry that I got suspended, and that I've brought shame to you and our family... But I'm not sorry about what I've done. He deserved it. Charlie is the most caring, loving human being I've ever met. And I will protect him until the day I die.

REVENGE

Rueben confronts his Mum about a secret she has been keeping from him for years.

RUEBEN. I am so angry at you right now. I can't even look at you.

Why would you do this to me? I don't get it! I'm fourteen for goodness sake, I could have handled the truth. But no, instead you've been lying to me for...seven years? Seven years Mum! What kind of example has that set? What kind of role model are you, eh? You're a joke. I have no respect for you now.

(He can't contain his anger.)

Do you realise how stupid I looked? Have you ever thought for one second what it would be like to stand in front of a group of people you know to hear, for the first time, that Dad is in prison? Yes, I overheard a conversation between two other parents. They were talking about Dad, knowing more about his life than I do. Me! His actual son. Do you know how humiliating that was? Do you?

(Pause. He is angry and emotional in equal measure.)

While all along you've painted this picture. Dad met someone else, dad moved away and left us. Do you know how screwed up that is? How screwed up that has made me? For years I've hated him with every ounce of me. Hated what he'd done to you. I go to bed every night wondering how he could have been so selfish. I beat myself up, thinking it must have been my fault, that I must have been too much for him. I forced him to leave. I beat myself up about that every single day.

Then I fantasise about what might happen if he came back, begging for forgiveness, asking to build a relationship with me again... While all along, this whole time - seven bloody years - he has been 30 miles down the road in the Abbey?

You've deprived me of a relationship with my Dad for seven years of my life. You're the selfish one. You're the one that needs to burn in hell.

How could you do this, Mum? How could you lie to me? How could you kill me like this on the inside?

You're not who I thought you were. What else have you lied to me about?

I can't look at you right now. I need to clear my head.

PIZZA PREDICAMENT

Millie has been forced to get a part time job. She is sharing her woes with her best friend, Emma.

MILLIE. Mum is making me get a part time job. Can you believe it?

I mean, as if I don't do enough already what with dancing and drama classes. I am out most nights of the week with barely any time to socialise as it is! And now she is demanding that I get a job and work myself to the bone. Honestly, I'll be heading for burnout very soon if she stays on my case.

The pizza place down the bottom of town offered me a job, because Mum knows one of the managers there, but what a disaster that turned out to be!

Get this. I went in on Monday for an 'induction' and they handed me a menu with nearly fifty pizzas on it, and told me to have it memorised for the next day! The pizza names, ingredients, prices. That's like a whole GCSE on its own.

Then, this guy in a dirty apron showed me how to *make* a pizza. How can I suddenly walk into the head chef role at a pizza joint when I can't even make a pot noodle at home? Like surely some Italian guy should be doing that, right? But it gets worse. When it came to my break, the owner smiled like a Cheshire cat, as if he was giving me a million pound, and said, *'Brucey Bonus! Each day you get to pick a pizza of your choice to have for dinner.'* My face said it all. Why would I want to eat a pizza every day? Is he trying to send me into obesity or what? I don't see that as a bonus and I haven't the foggiest who Brucey is. I wouldn't be surprised if him and my Mum had come up with some sort of agreement to kill me off quick. Imagine the headline:

"TEENAGER DIES AT DE-VINCI'S. PASSED
AWAY AMONG THE PEPPERONI. BODY
SLICED UP AND PUT IN A PIZZA BOX.

...Detectives on the hunt for 'Brucey'
character in connection with the murder."

Don't laugh Emma, this is a serious matter!
Needless to say - I didn't go back. I came out in floods of tears and begged Mum not to make me step foot in there ever again. When I got home though, I realised I'd left my blazer in the shop and poor Mum had to go back the next day to

collect it for me. I did feel bad. She was fuming, and embarrassed, and said I wasn't getting off the hook that easily. So, the search for a job continues.

Honestly, you'd think my Mum worked in a recruitment agency. I did say I'd love to help Miss Carol teach dance but apparently you need to have your final exam before you can do that ... *(Her phone rings.)*

(She mouths to Emma 'It's Mum'.) Hi Mum...I'm just about to start class, what's up? ...What? Are you serious? An old people's home? *Please* phone Di Vinci's and tell them I'll start tomorrow. And I'll have that menu learned off quicker than you can say...Margarita!

ROLLER COASTER

Ray tries to explain to a school counsellor how he has been feeling.

RAY. I'm finding this all a bit hard to explain. I know you've said that this is confidential, but I still feel, I dunno, weird. It's kind of strange to talk to a complete stranger about things you wouldn't say to your best mate. Do you get what I mean?

Anyway, I'm not good with words and shit, so it's hard.

Right, well, I dunno. I've just been feeling different this past while. About eight months really, to be more accurate. Just a bit up and down. One minute I'm normal and having a laugh with my mates, and the next I'm really depressed. Depressed is probably the wrong word. I'm not trying to say I've depression or anything. See, I told you I can't explain myself.

I suppose I just feel like I'm on a roller coaster. Yeah, that's what it feels like. At the weekends when I'm with my mates, everything's cool and fast-paced and fun. Then when I'm on my own again it feels like I've come down from a high, and everything has slowed down. That sounds wrong. I don't do drugs or anything. Jesus, you're probably going think I'm a junkie! *(He laughs.)*

What I'm trying to say is, that I always need something good to be happening for me to feel good. Whenever I'm on my own I think of loads of bad things. I have negative thoughts and shit, and it gets me down and makes me...makes me...you know, want to end it.

I've said too much. You're probably thinking I'm a bit of a dick. If my mates knew I was here, they'd laugh their heads off. (*Beat.*) But, I just thought, I dunno. I just thought maybe you'd be able to help?

CAROUSEL

Carousel explores the lives of five different young people who find themselves homeless. In this scene Luke speaks directly to the audience.

LUKE. My name is Luke. I'm sixteen. My mum kicked me out. Like, proper kicked me out.

Things have never been good, really. My dad left the scene when I was small. I don't remember him. And since then my mum has had a series of different men, none of them any good.

Most of them have been abusive; thrown their weight around, tried to lay down the law, that kind of thing. So we always came to loggerheads. I'm no angel, but I've always respected my mum - your mum's your mum at the end of the day. But her new flame of the month, well, he's in a different league. It's like he's some sick control freak, and the only way he knows how to respond to anything is with violence. I couldn't just sit there and watch him do that to my mum.

I gave her an ultimatum. "Him or me?" I said. "Him or me, mum?"

She chose him.

I started sofa surfing, around my mates' houses and stuff. Most parents just thought I was staying over, they hadn't a clue. But you can only do that for so long. It isn't a long-term answer. Friends' generosity only goes so far.

I ended up in a hostel trying to fend for myself. I don't feel like I've got a reason to wake up anymore. What is there to motivate me? No one's keeping me here. My mum doesn't want me anymore. What's the point in me getting up in the mornings? At the minute I'm made up of violence and anger.

It's like there's this bad person inside me and they're like stomping on the good bit that I know is in there. And I'm like "Get out!" I feel like there's this disease or this...infection inside me that makes me this way. All this bad stuff that's inside me, all this dirt...that I just need to get out.

I think deep down I am a good person, but it's deep, deep down in there.

I've tried to get the dirt away in every single way. I've tried jagging it away, I've tried snorting it away, I've tried drinking it away, I've tried fighting it away. I've tried slashing my own arms away.

I've tried everything to get it out. Nothing works.

MARKED

In this scene we meet seventeen-year-old Ross who explains the events of the night he was attacked.

ROSS. Saturday the fifteenth of February, cup final day. We played a blinder, beating Ardmore 4-1. I scored. One of those matches that will go down in history with your club. Everyone was on top form, celebrating and shit. We were all heading down to the club for pints, all the old hands were there, a proper 'knees up'. We could've been playing for a Premier League team and it wouldn't have been any better. I love it when everyone gets together, it's hard to beat.

Anyway, the club started to die down after about 9pm and so a few of us decided to head into town. We were all a bit rowdy but causing no harm to anyone. We went to 'Divine' nightclub at the end of Brennan Street. It's pretty new so I'd never been before. We queued to get in, got our stamp and away we went. The atmosphere was bouncing. We danced for a bit, got a few shots, danced a bit more.

Davey went to the toilet and I went to get another round of drinks. Davey seemed to be away for a while, but then I spotted him at the other side of the dancefloor talking to this big lad in a leather jacket. It didn't look friendly. I started to walk over, balancing the drinks in both hands. As I got closer I saw the big lad smack Davey in the face, it knocked him off his feet. I dropped the drinks and ran over, I was shouting at the guy to stop and I pulled him by the arm. He turned 'round and laughed in my face, then he got his drink and glassed me right here, below my eye. There was blood everywhere. I could feel the glass cutting into my face. He started punching me and completely knocked me out.

Obviously by then the bouncers intervened and me and Davey were brought to hospital. Davey had a swollen eye for a couple of weeks, and well, I'm scarred for life.

I've had two operations now and a bit of work done, but this is the best it's going to get. My face will look like this for the rest of my life.

The big lad's name was Jonny. Davey didn't even know him. He thought Davey gave his girlfriend a fly look and so he hit him a dig. I didn't know Jonny. Jonny didn't know me. Now I've to carry around a reminder of him for the rest of my life. Every time I catch myself in the mirror, there's no escaping that night.

ISSUES

Issues is a comic four-hander play which looks at the lives of four different characters who are all dealing with their own issues. Carl has just begun an anger management therapy group and shares his testimony for the first time.

CARL. Hi. My name is Carl. And I'm angry.

I've been angry now for...nine years. What makes me angry? Good question. Very good question.

It's just those doors. The doors that say push, only everybody pulls them. You know what I mean. Push. Pull. Push. Pull. Push. P.U.S.H. *(Mocking.)* "Oh, I'm so silly I just pushed the door and it says pull ... hehehe." I mean how hard is it? Push the thing!

It's not even that. It's... When you go to the cinema and the piece begins to build to this intense moment, and you're right there, captivated... Only some jerk is smacking on popcorn two rows up. It's infuriating! It makes you just want to turn around and punch the guy and keep punching him over and over and over until he stops. Surely you can relate to that?

Then there's those kids at school who revise the clock around, go in and sit the exam and come out in a tizz, saying how hard they'd found it and how they're sure to fail... Only guess what? Results come out, and what do you know? They get a top grade. Arrogant, egotistical idiots! They really make my blood boil.

Or...when you're seated beside some freak on an aeroplane who want to tell you their life story, in detail. When all you want to do is close your eyes and sleep. Or you're on a long-haul family trip to Florida, which is bad enough, and some baby screams the plane down the whole way there. There really should be a baby ban on flights. Seriously! It takes me every ounce of strength not to just...lash out and scream even louder than the damn baby!

Oh right ... sorry ... my time's up. No problem. Well, I'll just pull myself togeth- ...PULL! Push. Pull. Push.

I'll just... See you next week.

SCREAMING PIGS

Lucy is struggling to come to terms with the breakdown of her parents' marriage. Her mum has sat her down for a chat.

LUCY. I don't understand mum. I'm sorry, I don't. I don't want to move to another house. I love it here. This is where I grew up, this is where my friends are, this is my life. I don't want to change all that.

Do you know how long it has taken me to actually fit in? To make real friends, to feel popular? A pretty long time. Now you're telling me that we have to pack up and leave this all behind? Move to somewhere else and start brand new. Well, I don't want to. I'm sorry mum, I don't want to leave.

Surely things aren't that bad with dad? Can't you both work it out? Why can't we go back to the days when everything was normal? *(Beat.)* Do you wanna know the best day I ever had? It was a few years back, the weather was amazing, and you decided the three of us should pack up the car and head to the beach at Corney Bay? It wasn't planned, you hadn't organised it, you just looked out at the sun that morning and spontaneously thought, 'Let's go to the beach'. Do you remember? For once dad didn't hesitate or grumble and make a million and one excuses. He just smiled, like a proper smile, and he said, 'Let's do it'. You made sandwiches, packed buns and crisps and cheese, Dad put in our big red and green blanket and our swim gear and off we went.

Do you remember the three of us singing the whole way up? It was so silly, but we were all having so much fun together weren't we?

Then we got there, and dad buried me in the sand, it took him ages, but he never got bored or looked like he didn't want to do it. We went into the sea then, all three of us, because I was covered in sand, and we started jumping the waves. Then I remember dad grabbed you and pulled you in close and kissed you. And I remember thinking it was gross.

Well I don't any more. I wish we could just close our eyes and wake up back in that day. Stay in that moment.

Why does it have to change? Why can't we go back to what we were that day? I don't want to leave Mum, please don't make us.

THE WONDERFUL WEB

Natasha struggles with severe self-esteem issues. She often hides behind an online persona where she can pretend to be someone else. Someone that is accepted and liked. But in the silence of her own bedroom we see the real Natasha. A broken, vulnerable young girl crying out for help.

NATASHA. *(Seems upbeat as she sits at her desk on her laptop.)*

Now. Facebook login. Tori Tedford. It's got such a nice ring to it doesn't it? Tori has long brown hair and brown eyes, slim build and she's really, really popular. She is always checking in at the best places and sharing the most profound statuses. Tori is so cool! *(Beat.)* I love being Tori.

That's the advantage of the internet. You get to become who you want, chat to who you want and look whatever way you want. It's really simple when you know how. In school we always have these debates in English to help with our communication skills and they're always about the internet. Is

Facebook healthy for young people? Are young people spending too much time on the internet? Bla bla bla...

Well for me, I can honestly say it's great. I get to be who I want to be. Natasha Fitzpatrick can be 'somebody' for once in her life, somebody that matters.

(All of a sudden, we notice that Natasha's mood changes as she puts down the laptop. When she speaks the façade is gone and we see the real Natasha.)

If only it was like that in real life. If only I mattered to someone, anyone.

I'm that girl who sits her own, the strange girl that no one wants to bother with. I don't fit in. I'm an outcast.

My family have always been a bit dysfunctional, and I'm different. Look at me... (*She gets up and moves to the mirror, pulling her clothes and hair, etc.)* Nothing sits right on me and my hair is all over the place. No matter what I do or what I wear I can never get away from this. This thing that's staring right back at me in the mirror. This horrible thing that's called *me.*

I am so disgusting and ugly and fat. I can see why no one wants to be my friend, but I can't see what I can do about it. Every day I have to wake up like this - hating myself. Hating this big fat ugly mess that's me.

(She moves away from the mirror.)

That's the thing isn't it? About life. No matter what, you can never escape who you are, can you? There are self help books for this, that and the other; advice on how to overcome alcohol abuse, addiction, how to be a good parent, a good teacher, a good gardener! But I've never seen a book saying 'Ten steps on how to escape from being you'. It's one of those horrible things you're stuck with, isn't it?

I often think - why? Why they are the way they are, and me the way I am? How is it fair that God created everyone in the world, yet he made this big mistake with me and made everyone else so perfect. It's not fair. Life just isn't fair.

I hate waking up every day and having to do it all over again. Get dressed in my uniform, that looks so ridiculous on me; go into school where everyone glares at me and laughs; then come home and listen to Mum and Dad have another pointless row. I'm so tired, you know? So tired of pretending all the time. Sometimes I just want to open my mouth and scream at the top of my voice. But I'm worried that if I do that, I might never stop.

COLLA VOCE

Andrew is an accomplished, young opera singer. From an early age he showed great skill and has been nurturing his talent ever since. Andrew is rather eccentric and finds it difficult to relate to other young people and their interests, so tends to feel a bit isolated. His local town held a talent competition which he decided to enter, hoping that when people saw his passion for opera they might learn to understand and respect him more.

In this scene Andrew gives a statement to the police about the events of that night.

ANDREW. Okay officer, shall I start at the beginning?

Sure. Well, firstly I think it's important to point out that I'm an opera singer. I love the opera. I've grown up listening to opera and thank goodness my parents encouraged that and sent me along to a fabulous singing coach, with whom I've been working with since the age of seven. Opera is my life. If I'm not singing, I'm listening to music. It's my safe place, my haven, if you understand what I mean?

Anyway, I've always struggled to connect with my peers. At school, from quite early on, I knew I was different and I accepted that. I mean, I quite like who I am. I don't feel the need to change or succumb to what everyone else thinks a teenager should be doing. I'm not like the others, and quite frankly I don't want to be. Have you heard the music teenagers are listening to these days?

So, the evening in question, as you are aware, was the night of the talent competition in town. I thought it a lovely idea from the council. A wonderful way to bring the town together, a celebration. I toyed with the idea of entering initially, but then thought hey ho, you only live once. I naively thought that it might actually give me a bit of credibility with my peers. To help stop, you know, the constant verbal jabs at school.

After going through my repertoire with my singing coach we decided I should sing 'Se Vuol Ballare' from *'Marriage of Figaro.'* A stunning piece.

Tonight was my first ever public performance, and I loved it. The stage, the lights, the freedom of singing the words that I love. I couldn't see anyone. To me, the audience just looked like a sea of people with my voice, the tide rippling through them. It felt incredible. This was my moment and I seized it with both hands.

You know I came second, right? I was delighted with that. I mean, second in my first ever public performance? I felt like the world was at my feet. I felt untouchable, a cloud nine moment.

(Officer speaks.) Afterwards? Yes, I am coming to that now, officer.

There were hundreds of people about, masses of people, so Mum and I had arranged to meet back at the car. The car was parked in the car park behind Penbroke Street. So, I started to make my way back through the crowds. I decided to cut up through Loane Street as a shortcut. I was so excited to see my Mum, to share my joy, you know?

(Andrew is very uncomfortable sharing the next bit.)

I'm getting side-tracked again, sorry. So, in Loane Street I heard my name being called and when I turned around it was four guys from my school. I'd prefer not to share names if you don't mind. I thought that perhaps they wanted to congratulate me.

The next bit is quite uncomfortable to say, and I'd really prefer not to talk about it.

Sure, I know it's important that I do.

They came running towards me and surrounded me. They were shouting and chanting names at me. I really don't want to repeat the names. One of them punched me, right here in the eye as you can see, and then the others joined in kicking and punching, and pushing and shoving, until I was on the ground, in the foetal position begging them to stop.

I don't remember anything after that. I woke here, in hospital. I'd been knocked out, the doctor said. I've several bruises and three broken ribs. The doctor said I'm very lucky indeed, as my injuries could have been much more severe had the boys not been disturbed by the couple that were walking past. I really must make a note to thank them.

(Pause, then Andrew speaks softly and begins to break down.)

I've never felt fear like that before. Or pain. It started off with one blow then kept building and building and building. A bit like a Bartok symphony I suppose.

NOWHERELAND

Eighteen-year-old Lynne is struggling to come to terms with the death of her father. She has no contact with her mother and so her concerned boyfriend whom she lives with has asked her to sit down for a chat.

LYNNE. *(Snappy and sarcastic.)* Right. I'm here. You have my full attention, so go on, give it to me Craig. Tell me what's so important that we have to sit at the kitchen table for this counselling session? No, wait. I'll tell you, shall I? I mean, that's what the whole counselling concept is all about isn't it? Drawing the emotion out of your client.

Right well, here goes.

You're worried because you think I'm not coping. You think I'm drinking too much. Not eating enough. Blah blah blah. Okay Craig, I'll tell you what. I'll cut out down on the vodka, promise to eat my five a day, and meet you once a week around the kitchen table for a 'chat'. Happy?

(Beat.)

Sorry. I am sorry Craig, but I'm not a child. I'm fully aware of what's going on here. It's just hard.

I can't get it out of my head. It's not even the cancer... I mean, obviously it's the cancer, but what I'm trying to say is... That night. When we were told that he had basically, forty-eight hours to live and I stayed with him all night. I just held his hand telling him over and over again how much I loved him. I could tell he was fighting, you know, fighting to live because I was there with him.

But then...then I got tired. Tired! Do you realise how selfish that sounds? I got tired and I left him. Why did I do that? Why was I so selfish?

I just know in my heart that the minute I left that room he gave up. He stopped fighting and it's all my fault. He died alone. My dad died all alone and it's my fault.

I'll never forgive myself for that.

BREATHE

This play takes place in the aftermath of a tragic accident and explores how everyone copes very differently with the loss of a loved one. Libby's life has been propelled into a dark and lonely place.

LIBBY. Emma and I always got on. We didn't have one of those 'I hate my sibling' kind of relationships. With only two years between us, we were close, like best friends I guess. We did everything together. Even as kids, mum made us dress the same everywhere we went, and in a weird sort of way that never changed. We always borrowed each other's clothes, hung out with the same group of friends, and confided in each other about pretty much everything. It's such an advantage having an older sibling, they help pave the way for you and they've always got your back. Well that's how Emma and I were anyway.

Emma couldn't wait to get her test. She'd been practically saving her whole life for a car, and mum and dad always promised us that when we turned seventeen, they'd pay for lessons. I remember the day she passed her test, first time too. We went to Roma's to celebrate. Dad bought us a big slap up meal and we had chocolate fudge cake for desert.

Then the following week we started the search for a car. The budget was pretty tight but we narrowed it down to two cars. A bright yellow, sort of mustardy yellow Corsa, that had seen better days, but could be quite cool in a way. Or, a more traditional red Fiesta that was probably once sporty, in its day. Mum and dad preferred the Fiesta, but Emma and I thought there was something quirky about the Corsa, so that's what she decided upon. In our house we always made decisions together, we were funny like that. The four amigos.

Once all the paper work had been finalised, Emma got behind the wheel. For the first week or so, mum and dad only allowed her to drive from A to B to get used to the roads and stuff. The following week, Emma's friend was throwing a party to celebrate the end of exams and Emma persuaded mum and dad to let her drive there and back. Emma didn't drink or anything, so they were happy enough. Plus, Kelly, her friend only lived about 4 miles outside of town. I went along too.

Everything at the party was going great. A few of Emma's friends were having a drink and everyone was in great form, like animals let out of zoo for the day. Kyle, a guy that Emma was seeing at the time asked, "Right Emma, when are we all going to get a spin in your new wagon?"

And so, me, Emma, Kyle, Josh and Sophie went for a spin.

I remember the noise of the radio blaring out the best songs. I remember the laughs and screams of everyone, and how Josh kept shouting "faster, faster!" I remember the adrenalin, the excitement. I remember feeling free, cool, untouchable.

(Beat.)

Then I remember the crash, the impact, the screams. Car swerving, glass shattering, life slipping out of reach. I remember the silence that followed. That seemed to go on forever. Then people, sirens, movement, like a film playing before my eyes in slow motion.

I remember the blood, the pain, the ambulance.

I remember Emma. Lying meters away down the road. I remember seeing her lying lifeless, face down. I couldn't scream, I couldn't move, I was trapped inside a dream and all I could do was watch as everything unfolded in front of my eyes.

The ambulance rushed us away and I woke up later in a hospital bed with my Granny by my side, crying.

Emma died that night. She didn't stand a chance. She died at the scene and there was nothing anyone could do. Emma, my beautiful sister died at seventeen years of age, exactly two weeks after passing her driving test.

I remember every little thing in detail. I remember...but each day I pray that I'll forget.

SLASHED

Emily is a fifteen-year-old girl who hates P.E., and even worse...swimming. A teacher in school has discovered that Emily has been self-harming and has arranged for her to meet with the school counsellor. In this scene the school counsellor tries to encourage Emily to talk about what's worrying her.

EMILY. I did, I cut myself. No biggy. Nobody would have ever found out if we hadn't been forced to go swimming in P.E. Don't you think that's an issue you should be exploring? Maybe Miss Fraser should be in this seat next? Surely, in this day and age, going swimming should be a choice? Like, there are all sorts of girls, and boys for that matter, with more issues than me. Young people are body conscious, plus there's loads of bullying at the minute, people get tortured if they aren't the perfect body shape. And what do school do to support that? Send you to the bloody swimming pool where you have to parade about half naked in front of everyone! Great idea. Really productive for Year Tens.

Why do I do it? I dunno, why do you do what you do? People drink, take drugs, eat until they are obese... I cut myself. Same thing. Escapism. Simple as that.

I don't have to tell you how brutal the world can be, it's not pretty is it? Yeah, I could sit here and tell you all my problems, about why my dumb world is a sad and lonely place. But what's the point? Do you really care? Truthfully? You don't. And I'm fine with that. You're here cause it's your job, and you're getting paid for it. I get that. But I'm not going to pour out my life story to you. I don't feel the need to. Counselling won't work for me, I don't believe in it. Sorry if that offends you, but I don't.

So, yeah. When life gets crap, which tends to be a lot of the time, I cut myself until it hurts and I bleed. Then suddenly a new pain takes over my mind and body, and for that short period of time I'm free. I'm in control, and nobody can take that away from me. It's the only thing I've got.

SICK

Emma has been invited to Oakley High School to talk to a group of young girls about the reality of living with an eating disorder.

EMMA. Hi everyone. My name is Emma, which you probably already know. And I have bulimia. Which, I guess, you already know as well.

Anyway, I've been asked to come along today to talk to you about living with bulimia. So, I'm going to start at the beginning. Don't worry I promise not to go on for too long.

(Emma takes a drink of water and continues with a bit more confidence.)

When I was younger, I was confident and outgoing. I played all kinds of sport, went to dance class, gymnastics, the lot. I was quite popular and I was happy. When I reached high school, things started to change for me. My body started to change from a skinny kid to a curvy teenager. I guess I developed a bit quicker than most. Anyway, I didn't like the changes, they weren't welcome.

And I couldn't understand them. I wasn't suddenly eating loads of junk food or anything.

Anyway, I started to get hung up about this 'new me' and became very self-conscious. Of course, it wasn't just me that noticed the change, everyone at school did too. Primary school ended in June and I was a skinny thing; high school started in September and I'd become this curvy teenager suddenly. I hadn't seen many people over the summer holidays, so you can imagine everyone's reaction on that first week back at school. Kids can be so brutal.

At first, I stopped eating completely. I stopped dance classes, gymnastics, the lot. I didn't want anyone to see me in a leotard. I started to withdraw from social events, keep myself to myself. No one really noticed at first, but after a while my family figured me out.

So of course, mum and dad became obsessive about food. We had to sit round the table for every single meal, and I couldn't leave the table until my plate was cleared. Of course, they thought they were helping, by feeding me up. They never really asked me much about what was going on inside. They just thought that food was the answer. Little did they know, or understand, that food was the enemy.

That's when I started making myself sick. They may have been able to control what I ate, but they couldn't control what came up again. And that's where my story with bulimia began.

It didn't take long for it to spiral out of control. I don't want to bore you with all the details, they're not pretty. *(Starting to feel self-conscious.)*

Basically, I've lost over four stone, and as you can see I am seriously underweight. I have been hospitalised seven times now over the past few years, and the doctors says if I don't stop what I'm doing then...it could be life threatening.

(Beat)

You'd think that would make me stop, right? That's the thing. Bulimia gets a grip on you, such a hold over you that it suddenly doesn't become a choice anymore. At first, I felt great cause it was the one thing I could control. Now look at me. I'm a seriously ill seventeen-year-old who isn't physically fit enough to do anything with their life.

(Emotional, she pauses and takes another drink of water.) My advice to you is to love who you are. You may not be perfect. You may not look the way you'd want to, but trust me nothing is worth doing this to yourself. Nothing. At the moment, I'm taking my recovery one day at a time. I'm determined to get back to my old self, no matter how hard that may be.

TOUCH

Sophie voices her concerns to the youth leader, Sandra, about Nigel, the youth co-ordinator and manager of the community centre.

SOPHIE. It's probably nothing. I feel a bit stupid for coming to you about this. I've kind of put it off for weeks now, and don't really know if I'm making the right decision or not in talking to you.

(She takes a deep breath.) Okay. You know I've been coming to youth club since I was like, seven. How many years is that? (*Counting in her head.*) Eight years. Eight years I've been coming here. I've known Nigel a long time, and I love him to bits. What he has done for the community and for us kids has been amazing. The youth club has been the best part of growing up for me. I don't know where half of us would be without it.

The thing is though, with Nigel...he has always been a bit 'touchy feeley', if you know what I mean? Just with the girls. I know that he has an enormous amount of love to give, and maybe it's just that, maybe it is. But sometimes...sometimes, if I'm honest, I find it really inappropriate. And I know I'm not the only one. No one ever really talks about it, but the teenage girls all avoid him because we know what's coming.

Let me give you a few examples of what I mean. It's mostly unimportant things, like, he will hug all the girls, really tightly, but never ever does that to the boys. If you happen to be on your own with him the hug always seems to go on a few seconds too long, and it's a weird hug. Really tight, and he kind of moves his hands over your back.

Another example is that if he is talking to you about an issue or whatever, he always sits really close to you on the sofa in the common room, puts his hand on your leg and makes intense eye contact. It's creepy.

Last Friday night he heard Emily say that she had got her belly-button pierced and he went over to her and touched her belly, like her bare belly, put both his hands on her tummy and looked at the piercing. That weirded me right out!

That's sort of it, and it's probably not a big deal. I'm more than likely being paranoid. Or maybe it's me, maybe I'm the one with issues and don't like people invading my space or whatever. But I trust you Sandra, and it's been burning in me for ages to say something. I know the other girls feel the same way.

It's sad really, because we do all love Nigel. But as we've got older, it's got off-putting, and we all just try to avoid him. It's sad really.

BARE

Robyn is a seventeen-year-old girl who has just broken up with her long-term boyfriend. She speaks directly to the audience.

ROBYN. Darren and I broke up last week. I'm gutted to be honest. Two and a half years is a long time to spend with someone. It almost feels like a death. I know that's a morbid way to think of it, but it does. You spend so much time with one person, they get to know every little thing about you, and then, boom! They're out of your life.

In fact, if I'm being totally honest I think it's worse than a death. At least when someone dies, you don't see them again. I can't get away from Darren. We do go the same school, hang out with the same friends, socialise at the same places. How am I supposed to just casually see him and say hi, as if it's perfectly normal? And worse still, what if he moves on? Oh God, I can't even bare to think of that. I feel sick to my stomach at the thought.

I just never seen it coming, you know? He said some crap about us 'growing apart' and 'wanting different things', but both of us know the real reason. He broke up with me because I wouldn't have sex with him. Plain and simple. He's been trying for months, hinting about it, chancing his arm every time we were intimate together. Don't get me wrong, I'm not some sort of weirdo, we've done other things, but I'm just not ready for sex.

I know I'm seventeen and most people my age are doing it. I know we'd been together for years, but still, surely you should *feel* ready? I always imagine the first time to be so special and loving, I don't want to rush into it for the sake of it. It's not something you can ever re-live again, is it? Your first time should be perfect, and I just wasn't there with Darren yet. I probably would have been, through time, but obviously he didn't love me enough to wait! It's true what they say. Boys think with their... you know what. Now he'll probably go and sleep with the first girl he sees, and that'll tear me apart, it really will.

But I'm glad I held out, young people jump into bed with each other far too quickly these days! Oh no, I really do sound like my granny...but you know what I mean. I'm going to hold out until I feel ready, and I find the right person who'll want to be with me no matter how long that takes.

LOST AND FOUND

In this scene Matt is mourning the loss of his best friend Danny. Danny committed suicide, and this has left Matt feeling very lost and confused. He speaks his thoughts at Danny's graveside.

MATT. It's been two weeks now, mate and I'm still lost. I still can't make any sense of this. Why Danny, *why*? What were you hiding? What was going on that was so bad you couldn't tell me?

I just don't understand. I thought we told each other everything.

How could I not have seen there was something wrong with you? Was I too wrapped up in my own life to see that yours was falling apart?

I can't sleep at night. I play every detail of your life over and over in my head like a film, trying to look for clues, things I missed, that brought you to this. I can never find anything. You seemed so happy.

Just that afternoon we were planning things. We were talking about getting tickets for the match, heading to Murray's party, scheming about the formal. You seemed so normal, so up for it, so you.

Not one single thing seemed out of place with you. In fact, you actually seemed happy? I'll never get that.

I'll never forget your mum phoning me, the sound of her voice, her squeals. I couldn't make sense of what she was saying. It felt like her words were coming at a hundred miles an hour, but my thoughts were in slow motion. I couldn't accept what she was saying. I still can't accept it.

No warning, no reason, no goodbye. So final. You didn't leave us anything mate. No note, no clue. We're all just left with unanswered questions. All of us searching and searching, retracing your last steps, replaying your last words, but coming up with nothing. Nothing at all.

Didn't you think about how this would leave us all? None of us will ever be the same again.

We loved you mate, we loved the bones off you. Your family, your mates, Clarissa, all of us. We bloody well loved you mate. Couldn't you see that?

What did we do? What happened to you Danny? Show me mate, show me please.

BRUISED

Caitlyn speaks to her best friend Chloe about the previous evening.

CAITLYN. I feel so sick Chloe. Not just physically sick, but worried sick. How did I get into that shape? I didn't drink much more than I usually do. That's the first time ever that I don't remember a thing. My last memory is at about eleven last night, and we didn't get back here until half one in the morning...? That's two and half hours that I've lost. What the hell? That's crazy. I could have done anything in that time and I wouldn't even know about it. How can I face everyone Chloe? Like, ever again? I don't know what I've said, what I've done... and I'm way too paranoid to look at my phone. I just can't bring myself to do it. Not even an option.

Here's the worst part. My very last memory is of me chatting to Stevie in the wee booth thing beside the bar. I remember feeling really confident and flirty. I remember him saying that he would be interested in me if he wasn't going out with

Chelsea. I remember saying something along the lines of "What she doesn't know won't hurt her..." *Why* would I say that? I really like Chelsea.

Anyway – boom - that's my last memory. I have no idea what happened after that. Did he tell me to clear off? Did I force him to cheat on his girlfriend? Did we kiss? Did we have mad sex in the bloody toilets? I don't know! I could have done anything, and I don't know! I am never drinking again. This is awful. I can't leave the house or talk to anyone ever again. I just want to curl up and die.

(Chloe responds.)

I am *not* being dramatic Chloe. I have lost hours of my life that I will never get back, and I could be like...fifteen hours pregnant and not even know about it. *(This realisation dawns on her.)* Oh God. I could be pregnant. I'm going to be sick.

(She rushes off to throw up.)

THE CURRENT

Reece is reeling from the aftermath of an ill-fated camping trip with his friends. His close friend Jess tragically lost her life in an accident.

REECE. What is there to say? No words sound right in my mouth. Everything feels like an excuse, a justification. But the reality is, Jess is dead and it's all our fault. We're responsible. She's dead, and we're to blame. Our friend is gone, and we can't do anything, anything at all to bring her back.

Why did life have to do this? Is there even a God in the sky?

It feels like there is a dark cloud over my world, and it's never going away. Everyone looks at me and points and whispers. No one understands. None of us speak anymore. Clare made it pretty clear she hates me. I tried phoning and texting Burnsey. I called at his door, but no. He's dropped out of school and won't see anyone.

I'm seeing a counsellor and that does help. It helps me to understand my thoughts, organise them. But nothing will ever help this feeling I have inside. This feeling of emptiness, of nothingness. Sometimes it actually feels like my heart is breaking in two, it feels sore, incurable. In one night I lost everything. I lost Jess. I should have had more sense. They were drunker than I was, but I still went along with it. I wanted to keep up with Burnsey. I put my own ego before the safety of my friends. Then I just became as stupid as they were. If only I could turn back time to when life made sense.

I had her hand...I had her hand in my hand... and I let go. How could I have let go? I will never forgive myself. Never.